The Seven
Circles of Prayer

The Seven Circles of Prayer

By John Wijngaards

McCRIMMONS
Great Wakering Essex

Father John Wijngaards worked in India for 15 years. He was Vicar General of the Mill Hill Missionaries, and is now Director of Housetop Centre in London. He has written many books, including *Experiencing Jesus, Biblical Spirituality* and *Communicating the Word of God.*

First published in Great Britain in 1987 by
McCrimmon Publishing Co Ltd
Great Wakering Essex England

ISBN 0 85597 400 1

Cover photograph: Jackie Clackson
Typeset by Barry Sarling Rayleigh Essex
Printed by Mayhew McCrimmon Printers Ltd
Great Wakering Essex

Contents

Foreword

This booklet is meant for you if you seek to meet God in prayer. You can use it in conjunction with our Housetop video, *The Seven Circles of Prayer*. Or you can read it on its own.

Prayer of the heart, 'inner prayer', is something very personal. Every one of us, whether man or woman, young or old, has to find his or her unique path to God. But we can learn from other people. There are common elements that feature in all mature prayer. In this booklet I distinguish seven which I propose as seven concentric circles through which everyone should pass to meet Christ in the centre. Chapter One describes these seven steps in simple terms.

Prayer offers no escape from our world. Prayer opens our eyes and our ears so that we can reach out to other people with empathy and love. In particular, prayer makes us aware of human suffering; of hurts requiring our healing touch. I meditate on this in the second chapter.

The third and final chapter gives examples of how our encounter with Christ can take place in the midst of our urbanised and secular living. Christ promised he would make himself known (Jn 14,18-23). 'You will not be left alone. I will reveal myself to you,' he said.

The seven circles

You can start from any point on the outside.
The way in will be the same for all.

Chapter One

A method of praying

Over the centuries saints and mystics have worked out various approaches to prayer. These approaches differ from each other in a number of ways, but they also have certain elements in common. In this booklet, no less than in our video programme of the same title, I have put together those common elements in a coherent form. Basing myself on my own experience and on what I found in spiritual classics, I am suggesting this as a simple method that could make prayer a reality in your everyday life. I am sure that this will help you become a different person, better equipped to face the challenges that come your way.

1. Seek moments of silence

Our everyday life is filled with noise. Noise from outside: running engines, traffic, radio and television, conversations with friends, colleagues, customers... Internal noise: our hobbies and distractions, work done under pressure to meet deadlines; worries and concern. Sometimes we get so used to all this 'noise', that periods of enforced silence fill us with boredom and fear.

But if we want to attain awareness of reality, if we want to transcend the flow of trivialities, if we want to understand the things that really matter, we have to learn to withdraw to silence. Silence actually is a beautiful thing. It is pure like fresh air in the mountains, like water in a clear spring. All religious traditions stress this need of withdrawal: whether this implies going into a retreat, living in isolation as monks do, or having fixed periods of reflection, time set aside for oneself and for God.

It is essential therefore that you find time in your daily schedule for silence. In practice this will mean two things. First, you will not spoil the natural moments of silence that come your way: as when you are travelling, when you are washing up, when you are doing certain actions that allow your mind silent concentration. Secondly, at least once a day you will set aside fifteen minutes to half an hour for explicit withdrawal in 'inner prayer'. Once you have acquired the habit you will find it so rewarding that you will not like to miss this period of the day. Some people find the morning best, before going to work; others prefer the evening. Whatever time it is, make sure that it is a time when you can switch off all outer and inner noise.

Large crowds used to gather to listen to Jesus and seek cures from their diseases. But Jesus had the custom of going to lonely places where he could pray. (Lk 5,15-16)

At that time (the day before choosing the Apostles) Jesus went out into the hills to pray. He spent the whole night there praying to God. (Lk 6,12)

2. *Pause on your journey*

Everything in this world is constantly changing and moving. The earth turns round. All living beings, including ourselves, grow and die. Nature changes from one cycle to the next. Autumn becomes winter; spring changes into summer. Everything is on the move.

We may rightly consider our own life as a journey. We are travelling all the time, but, humanly speaking, our point of departure and our destination are not so clear. It is as if the road behind us and the road in front of us are shrouded in a deep fog. Who am I? Where do I come from? What is the purpose of my journey? Am I, perhaps, losing my way?

It is obvious that in such a human condition we cannot afford to simply walk on blindly. We have to sit down and take our bearings. We express this symbolically, but very meaningfully, by choosing a convenient place and a posture of 'rest' for our inner prayer.

In one way the place of prayer is not important. We can withdraw into ourselves and pray anywhere. But experience has shown that it helps our inner prayer if we select the right place for it. This is also the reason why in practically all religious traditions special places were set aside for this purpose like churches, synagogues, temples and so on.

In your own case I suggest that you select some special spot where you feel really at home and at rest. You may want to sit cross-legged on the floor. Or you may feel more comfortable in an armchair. Then again you may prefer to stroll leisurely in a quiet corner of the park. Whatever you do, your place and your posture should express not only your withdrawal from noise but also your withdrawal from movement.

When you pray, go into your room, close the door and pray to your Father on your own, in secret. And your Father who sees whatever happens in secret, will make it worth your while. And in praying do not use a lot of empty words as pagans do who believe God will listen to them because their prayers are long. Do

not be like them. Your Father knows what you need
even before you ask him. (Mt 6,6-8)

3. Observe deeper realities

Suppose you are in your favourite place of prayer.
First, you withdraw from all the noise inside and
outside of you. Then, when everything has become
quiet in you, you focus your eyes on the deeper
realities you have come across in the course of the
day. Let me explain to you what this means.

There are different ways of looking. There are
degrees of seeing reality. If a man walks through the
forest, he may be so preoccupied with himself or his
work that he will only notice the path which he is
following. But if he has time to look around and
observe, he will notice also how beautiful the trees
are. He may wonder at their variety, at the colours of
green and brown they exhibit, at the power of life in
them, and so on. He may suddenly see there is something undefinably wonderful in the forest,
something that lies on the borderline of our perception. In other words, he may become aware of a
mystery, of dimensions that go beyond what we can
see with our eyes. Where does this beauty come
from? How does my life take part in the life of these
trees?

What is really happening is that he is not only
seeing the trees themselves as things or objects, he
sees them as 'symbols', as signs of Reality as such, of
deeper reality. This ability to see the symbolic
nature of things is something we gradually acquire
by being open to it. It is in order to strengthen this
sense of perception, incidentally, that various religious traditions use symbols and signs: such as
religious vestments, decorations in church, incense,

186,000 m/sec

1 light year = 365 × 186,000 × 60 × 60 × 24 miles

Nearest star

V = speed of light

1. Set aside time
2. Choose a place
3. Recapture moments of
   truth encounters during the
   day

and so on. It helps to develop our sense of deeper perception.

Or imagine a woman doing her shopping in a supermarket or teaching children in a comprehensive school. Instead of just getting the job done, she might look at people's faces, remembering that each is an individual, with fears and hopes. Suddenly she starts seeing them in a new way. They become persons to her. In fact, by noticing the uniqueness and dignity in each, she may become aware of the inexpressible Person of which we are all a created image.

During your time of inner prayer, recapture the moments of such observation you have had in the course of the day or on previous occasions. By reflecting on it for some time, you sharpen your sense of observation. In the silence of your place of spiritual rest, try to become acutely aware of the mysterious, wider dimensions of your existence. These wider dimensions, you will realise, disclose to you the presence of 'God' — the ultimate ground of your being, the creator and cause of all reality. You will also begin to love people in a new way.

Early one morning Elisha's servant got up, went outside and saw that a Syrian army with horses and chariots had surrounded the town. Returning to his master, he cried: 'We are doomed! What shall we do?!' 'Don't be afraid!', Elisha answered. 'Our troops are more numerous than theirs.' Then he prayed, 'Lord, please, open his eyes so that he can see.' Then the Lord opened the eyes of the young man. He saw, to his surprise, that the hillside was covered with horses and chariots of fire. (2 Kings 6,15-17)

4. Hear the cry of people's suffering

Just as our sense of sight needs to be refined, so it is with our sense of hearing. We hear lots of things, but usually we have not learned to really listen. When people speak to us, we pay attention only to the immediate meaning of their words, without listening to the underlying message. A person may come to us with some neighbourly gossip; her real need may be loneliness and lack of encouragement. When we carry sufficient silence in our heart, we will notice the underlying message too. Then we will meet suffering.

During your period of inner prayer, make time for such 'interior listening'. This means that you go back to all the things you heard, people speaking to you at home or at work, communication from the press, radio, TV, and so on. You listen again to the things you heard, but now with renewed attention to the deeper, underlying messages. Often it will confirm what you already knew from your 'seeing'. Often it will mean that you will hear people cry in anguish. You will become more aware of what their real needs are, of what they are trying to tell you.

As you develop this sense of hearing, you will automatically react in a number of ways. You will become more conscious of your own hardness of heart, your prejudices and other failings towards others. You will feel sorry about this, and perhaps make up your mind to amend. You will also want to help those in need. You will bless them in your heart; you will intercede for them with God, asking that God may bless them. And you will, no doubt, decide to take some responsibility for them, if it lies within your power.

The Lord said: 'I have seen the affliction of my

14

people in Egypt. I have heard them cry out in anguish, because of their slave-drivers. I know how much they suffer. That is why I have come down to free them from slavery to the Egyptians and to take them to a spacious, rich and fertile land.' (Exodus 3,7-8)

5. Heal by your touch

Our human skin is one of the most wonderful organs we possess. Not only does it protect us from external pressures and regulate our temperature, it is covered with millions of small receptors by which we can feel physical reality around us. The skin is also the organ by which we most directly experience what care and tenderness mean. It is through our skin that we first learn love: when our mother touches us.

In all our relationships this sense of touch remains very important throughout life. Even in those cases where we do not touch another person physically, our sensitivity or lack of it plays a great role. Sensitive people are constantly aware of how their words and actions may hurt other people, and how their gentleness and respect will heal and encourage.

During your time of inner prayer review your relationships with friends, relatives, and people you work with or work for. Allow your feelings to come to the surface. How have you been 'in touch' with them? Perhaps there is need of reconciliation, of a gentler approach, of greater sensitivity...Reach out to them. Surround them with love. Social custom may restrict the extent you will be able to express your love by a physical touch. But no one can stop you 'touching' people's hearts; by a gesture, a word of encouragement, the gift of your time, or whatever may be required.

A woman who had suffered from a bleeding came up behind Jesus. She touched the fringe of his mantle; for she thought: 'If I can only touch his clothes, I will be cured.' Immediately her bleeding stopped. She felt in her body that she was healed of her illness. Jesus had noticed that power had gone out from himself. He turned round to face the crowd and said: 'Who touched me?' His disciples protested: 'Don't you see that many people are pressing around you? How can you say: "Who touched me?" ' But he looked around to spot the person who had done it. Fully aware of what had happened, the woman stepped forward in fear and trembling. Falling at his feet she told the whole truth. 'Daughter,' Jesus said to her, 'your faith has made you well. Go in peace. Be healed of your trouble.' (Mk 5,27-34)

A note in between

In the preceding five sections I have outlined aspects of our inner prayer which are of a general nature. Even though they are Christian in inspiration, they reflect similar practices in other religions. Any religious person seeking to pray, whatever religion he or she belongs to, can join in without feeling embarrassed or inhibited.

In the next two sections I will indicate the elements that are specifically Christian.

6. Respond to the Word of life

We, Christians, believe that God has revealed himself to us. He has made himself known as a God of love. He invites us to become his beloved sons and daughters if only we accept the gift of his friendship with faith. Our Christian prayer is therefore not only a response to God as he shows himself to us in created reality and in people around us; it is also a response to his life-giving message.

16

That is why Sacred Scripture is so important to us. In it God himself speaks. Through many stories and images we can learn what he expects from us. The Bible is a living word that needs to be interpreted by every person according to one's own context and circumstances. Our response to the world in which we live receives a new dimension by our reflection on God's word.

In practice this means that the reading of a Scripture text and reflection on it should be a normal part of your inner prayer. It may be a good idea to put it usually rather at the beginning of your meditation time. After withdrawing in silence, you might want to start with a Scripture passage and reflect on it. Then you could turn to the other steps of your response: observing deeper realities, hearing people's cry, reviewing the touch of your relationships. You will find that your scriptural insight will not fail to throw a new light on these different aspects of your inner prayer.

Jesus went to the synagogue as his custom was on the sabbath day. He stood up to read and was handed the scroll of the prophet Isaiah. He opened the scroll and looked for the place where it is written: 'The Spirit of the Lord is upon me...' He closed the scroll, gave it back to the attendant and sat down. The eyes of all in the synagogue were fixed on him. 'This passage of Scripture, as you heard it read, has come true today,' he said. (Lk 4,16-21)

7. Meeting Christ face to face

The core of our Christian belief is that God became visible to us in Jesus Christ. In him God has come really close. It is as if God, who remains such a mystery as the ground of our being and the ultimate reality of the universe, has shown us his 'face'. He has become a person we can talk to, a close friend, a dear father.

We saw that there are various aspects of inner prayer which we have in common with all religious people. This nearness of God in Christ provides new meaning to those aspects. Our awareness of deeper realities manifests itself in a special way in our participation in the sacraments. In these religious symbols we see Christ at work; at the Eucharist he becomes truly present. When we hear people cry in anguish or hope, we realise it is Jesus Christ, our brother, who is crying out in them. When we touch other people around us, we do so with even greater love and respect because we remember that what we do to them we do to Christ. You will find this worked out more fully in Chapter Two: 'Awareness of the Suffering Christ'.

True Christian inner prayer will soon become a prayer of Christ awareness. Prayer becomes an encounter. Be prepared for this change in your prayer. It is with Christ and through Christ that you will address yourself ever more confidently to the Father. By your recollection and your loving concern for other people, you open yourself fully to Christ's Spirit so that he can transform you and show you how you should live. Ask Christ that he may make you aware of the various ways he shows himself to you. You can read more about this in Chapter Three: 'The Moment of Encounter'.

'In the future, the world will not be able to see me, but you will see me. Because I am alive, you will have life. Then you will know that I am in my Father; that you are in me and I in you. A person who holds on to my commandments (of love) and puts them into practice, loves me. My Father will prove his love to whoever loves me. I too will love that person and make myself known to him or her.' (Jn 14,19-21)

Chapter Two

Awareness of the suffering Christ

A Meditation[1]

The high priest stood up in the sanhedrin and asked Jesus: 'Have you no answer to make?' But Jesus 'was silent and made no answer' (Mk 14,61; Mt 26,63). While Jesus was in Herod's court, he maintained the same silence. The scribes accused Jesus vehemently. Herod questioned him at length. His courtiers ridiculed and mocked him. But Jesus 'made no answer' (Lk 23,9). Pilate too was exasperated by Jesus' reticence. 'You will not speak to me? Do you not know that I have power to release you and power to crucify you?' But apart from an occasional word, 'Jesus gave no answer' (Jn 19,9). Neither did he give an answer to the Pharisees who derided him during the crucifixion. His only reply was the prayer, 'Father, forgive them' (Lk 23,34). Jesus' silence is a datum of ancient tradition firmly embedded in the passion accounts.

The early Christians recognised in this one more feature of that suffering servant whom they knew to be Jesus. 'As a sheep led to the slaughter or a lamb before its shearer is dumb, so he opens not his mouth' (Is 53,7-8; Acts 8,32-35). But the silence of Christ is not a later construction to fit the prophecy.

The inner cohesion of Christ's silence with other events in the passion story demonstrates this. It is also abundantly clear from the way Peter refers to the fact. In the context of instructing Christians to suffer patiently, he naturally turns to the example of Christ. After quoting the words of Scripture 'No guile was found on his lips' (Is 53,9), he goes on in his *own* words: 'When he (Jesus) was reviled, he did not revile in return; when he suffered he did not threaten; but he trusted him who judges justly' (1 Pet 2,23). Christ's actual behaviour is the model for Christians: 'Christ suffered for you, leaving you an example that you should follow in his steps' (1 Pet 2,21). This prophecy is explained by Christ's factual behaviour and not vice versa.[2]

The Fathers of the first centuries take issue with Jesus' silence in different ways. Their main concern appears to have been the fear that it might be mistakenly understood as an admission of guilt. In Roman antiquity judicious silence was praised, but not silence as such: *Nemo silens placuit* ('Nobody has been received well by silence').[3] 'The silent seems to express agreement'.[4] 'A stupid man keeping silent may be reckoned to be wise'.[5] Against such possible misconstruing the Fathers rise in defence. 'Jesus sometimes *did* give an answer', says Augustine. 'But as the comparison with the lamb that is slaughtered shows, he kept silent not as one convicted of evil but as an innocent person, in all his meekness to be sacrificed for the sins of others'. Chrysostom remarks, 'Replying would have been useless. It was only a make-believe trial. In reality Jesus was attacked by robbers'. Origen asks, 'Why should he answer those who had put up self-contradicting witnesses against him?' Jerome goes even further: 'Silence was fitting to the majesty of Jesus. Those judges were unworthy of an answer.' Modern authors concur with this line of interpretation when they attribute

Jesus' silence to some kind of court strategy: by not giving an answer Jesus wanted to force his opponents to advance the real reasons for which they wanted Jesus killed.[6]

However valid the above interpretations may be, they are too superficial to do justice to the terrifying reality of Christ's silence. Gregory the Great was nearer to sensing its full import when he remarked:

'If people praise us for our talk but are not ready to change their wrong ways, it is better to keep silent. Otherwise we obtain a share in their wrong doing since they praise our words but don't follow them.'

Even if it is somewhat inadequately expressed, we find here the realisation that Christ's attitude of silence transcended the immediate circumstances of his passion. Gregory sensed that Christ was loyal to his character and his words by adopting this attitude.[7]

Much more penetrating than all this has been the thought of Ignatius of Antioch. In his letter to the Ephesians he put down the kernel of a real theology of the silence of Christ. Ignatius had been struck by the contrast between the intrinsic importance of salvific events and their lack of publicity. He speaks of the 'silence of God'.[8]

'Hidden from the prince of this world was the virginity of Mary and her child-bearing and likewise also the death of the Lord — three mysteries to be cried aloud — the which were wrought in the silence of God.' (Eph 19)

Ignatius sees the same silence at work in the life of Christ:

'It is better to keep silent and to be, than to talk and not to be. It is a fine thing to teach, if the speaker practise. Now there is one Teacher who spoke and it came to pass: yes, even the things he has done in silence are worthy of the Father. He that truly possesses the word of Jesus is able also to hearken unto his silence, that he may be perfect: that through his speech he may act and through his silence may be known.' (Eph 15)

Lightfoot maintains that the immediate cause for Ignatius to utter these words was the circumstance that the bishop of Ephesus, Onesimus, was a quiet person, rather reticent and withdrawn.[9] Ignatius, who had been much impressed by the bishop (Eph 5) may have seen in him a living example of the 'silent Christ'.

'In proportion as a man sees that his bishop is silent, let him fear him the more... We ought to regard the bishop as the Lord himself.' (Eph 6)

Whatever the occasion, the fact remains that Ignatius was struck by 'the silence of Christ'. He recognised it as an important way in which Christ communicated with his followers. 'Even the things Christ did in silence are worthy of the Father.' Did Ignatius think of Jesus' hidden life? Or did he refer more particularly to his suffering? 'He that truly possesses the word of Jesus is able also to hearken unto his silence.' What is this 'silence of Jesus' that the believer should listen to? Is it the silence of Christ as expressed in the Gospel narratives? Or does it include other present-day forms of silence in which Christ manifests himself? If the silent bishop of Ephesus made the silence of Christ a contemporary reality for Ignatius, in what other ways can the silence of Christ be heard? And should it be listened to?

The silence of God

When Almighty God did not listen to the prayer of an innocent man and allowed the wicked to pursue their evil course, God was occasionally said to be 'silent' (Heb 1,13; Ps 28,1; 50,21; 35,22; Is 57,11; 65,6). In such cases the delay of saving intervention on God's part was considered an unusual and exceptional occurrence. It happened. But the conviction was that it happened rarely and it should not happen. The silence of God was considered to be essentially of limited duration.

The real theologian of God's silence in the Old Testament is Kohelet. Even though he never uses the word, the idea is an integral part of Kohelet's thought. Kohelet was a realist. Where other religious leaders mouthed platitudes, he stated the blunt truth. Kohelet was haunted by the riddle of human existence, by its soberness and harshness, by the utter uselessness of human effort, by the obvious contradiction between religious promise and everyday reality. As far as human observation goes, the saintly person suffers and dies just as the sinner. 'The wise man dies just like the fool.' (Koh 2,17)

'Everything before men is useless, since one fate comes to all, to the righteous and the wicked, to the good and the evil, to the clean and the unclean, to him who sacrifices and him who does not sacrifice.' (Koh 9,1b-2)

The unprejudiced observer will note that man dies like an animal.

'For the fate of the sons of men and the fate of beasts are the same: as one dies so dies the other.' (Koh 3,19)

Worst of all, during persecution, war, rape and murder it is brute power that wins the upper hand. An objective observation of human events forces on one the conclusion that for some people life is simply unbearably cruel.

'Again I saw all the oppressions that are practised

under the sun. And behold, the tears of the oppressed and they had no one to comfort them! On
the side of their oppressors there was power, and
there was no one to comfort them (the oppressed).
And I thought the dead who are already dead more
fortunate than the living who are still alive. But
better than both is he who has not yet been, and
has not seen the evil deeds that are done under the
sun.' (Koh 4,1-3)

Kohelet knows God to be responsible for this world.
God is the creator (Koh 12,1). Everything on earth is
'the work of God who makes everything' (Koh 11,5).
God gives man life, possessions and honour if he
wishes to do so (Koh 5,19; 6,2); but it is also God
who has given to man all the 'unhappy business'
man is forced to be busy with (Koh 1,13). It is God
who made the world the way it is. 'Who can make
straight what God has made crooked?' (Koh 7,13; 1,15)
   Kohelet realises that God must have had a purpose
in all he did. But for some appalling reason God has
not revealed this to man. Surrounded by a mad
world, man gropes in utter darkness. 'That which is,
is far off, and deep, very deep; who can find it out?'
(Koh 7,24). Man takes decisions without knowing
what they will lead to. 'For who knows what is good
for man while he lives the few days of his useless life
which he passes like a shadow?' (Koh 6,12a) Man
marches through life but may be snatched up by
death at any unexpected moment. 'Man does not
know his time' (Koh 9,12). And what will happen
after death? Kohelet sees but darkness and uncer-
tainty (Koh 3,21; 6,12b; 8,7; 9,10).

'When I applied my mind to know wisdom and see
the business that is done on earth, how neither day
nor night one's eyes see sleep, then I saw all the
work of God that man cannot find out, the work
that is done under the sun. However much man
may toil in seeking, he cannot find it out. Even

24

though a wise man claims to know, he cannot find
it out.' (Koh 8,16-17)

'Who can tell man how it will be? (Koh 6,12b; 8,7)
Only God could, if he wished to do so. But God
maintains silence. God deliberately decided not so
speak. Kohelet makes no bones about it. God makes
us realise his power by his silence. 'God is in heaven
and you are upon earth' (Koh 5,2). 'God is testing
the sons of men to show them that they are but
beasts' (Koh 3,18).

'God has put eternity into man's mind, yet so that
he cannot find out what God has done from the
beginning to the end.' (Koh 3,11)

Is it not remarkable and stimulating to find such
words as the above recorded in inspired writing? In
our endeavour to harmonise and reconcile, to 'plead
the case for God' (Job 13,8), we tend to by-pass and
obscure the terrifying silence of God. The world is
more a madhouse than a home. God allows man to
stumble in the dark. God keeps silent where he could
speak. It is true, the revelation of his plan of love
through Jesus Christ has lifted a tip of the veil. It has
let through a glimmer of hope. But by and large the
silence of God has not been broken. Alongside his
word we find a void of speech. Alongside the
message of Christ we find his silence.

Listening to Christ's silence

Christ's silence at his passion and the theology of
Kohelet, seemingly unconnected, point to a manner
of experience of Christ which appears to be both
factual, of crucial value to our times and yet frequently overlooked. It is my contention that Christ
is in many ways communicating to us through his
silence, but that we do not heed his message.

Let me from the outset eliminate some other

meanings that could be given to the term 'the silence of Christ', and which are not intended by me in the context of this meditation. All great Christian mystics, with pseudo-Dennis the Areopagite, Ruysbroeck, St John of the Cross and St Thomas Aquinas as their spokesmen, have always maintained that the higher stages of contemplation and mystical union with God require intellectual and emotional bonds that go beyond concepts and expression. God is met ultimately in a 'cloud of unknowing', in a 'dark night', in the 'super-essential radiance of the divine obscurity'. Christ and the soul are then enveloped in an 'unutterable silence', a silence that goes beyond words, carrying as it does a reality that transcends human language.[10] This silence, related though it may be, is not the one intended by me in this study. I would also like to exclude the more common understanding of the term as spiritual desolation. Persons undergoing spiritual aridity in prayer sometimes speak of Christ being silent to them.[11] This silence also falls outside our immediate scope.

Communication analysts have come to accept the principle that a human being, if present to another human being, cannot not communicate with him.[12] By our very make-up we *have* to communicate. If we don't speak, it is our silence itself that communicates. Thus it is with Christ. In the sanhedrin, in Herod's court, before Pilate's judgement seat and on Calvary he was there for all to see. He moved in the focus of the action. His personality dominated the scene. But 'He was silent'. It seems to me that Christ's silence demands our response whenever he makes his presence strongly felt but without speaking. It is this reticent and mute, but forceful, presence of Christ I understand to be his silence.

Kohelet was confronted with the silence of God mainly in the agony of his fellow human beings. He saw 'the tears of the oppressed' (Koh 4,1), the darkness, grief, vexation, sickness and resentment of the common man (Koh 5,17). He observed how the 'righteous perish in their righteousness'. He was shocked because he knew God to be there: 'I know it will be well with those who fear God' (Koh 8,12). Kohelet was appalled by God's silence precisely because it was God himself who made the day of adversity (Koh 7,14). It was not the absence of God that troubled him, but the awful presence of the silent God.

Kohelet might have been even more troubled if he had known, as we do, that God was to identify himself fully with the oppressed in Jesus Christ: 'I was hungry and you gave me no food' (Mt 25,42). As I am writing these words, more than a thousand delegates from many nations are gathered in Rome for the World Food Conference sponsored by the United Nations. The din of discussion on calorie intake, fertilisers, world food banks, agricultural economics and the Green Revolution cannot obliterate the agonising silence of emaciated millions who cannot even ask for the food they need. The silence of Christ stares at us from the faces of the famished. The same amount of food that is feeding one average rich person, nutritionists point out, can feed a whole family of seven on an average poor man's diet.[13] If I am rich and don't share till it hurts, I can justify my action with words, but I can never escape the silence of Christ.

The silent Christ is with us every day. In people who are bereaved, who are sad and depressed, who are upset and confused, it is Christ calling out to his Father in Gethsemani. Whenever the poor are robbed by those in power, when minorities are marginalised, when people's rights are trampled under foot, Christ stands in court with no one to defend him. The tears of those who are suffering pain mingle with Jesus' sweat and blood trickling down from the cross on Golgotha. If we come close, we can hear him speak. 'Father, if it is possible, let this chalice pass me by.' 'God, my God, why have you forsaken me?' And: 'Whatever you do for the least of mine, you have done for me.'

Chapter Three

The moment of encounter

Christ may reveal himself to us at a time when we least expect him to. Saul met him on the way to Damascus and Simone Weil was overwhelmed by Christ's presence at Solesmes before she realised such a thing could ever happen. There is an element of the unexpected in every self-communication of God, even though Christ's promise prepares us for it. Love works with surprises.[14]

On the other hand, there are certain situations that seem to lend themselves more readily to channelling a Christ-experience. Some have been indicated by Christ himself or by the Gospels as being particularly favourable. Others can be deduced from the experience of saints and mystics. Knowing what these situations are may make us more sensitive to Christ's presence if and when he decides to communicate with us through them.

In this chapter I will indicate seven such situations. Although all have their prototypes in the Gospel, they were selected mainly because of their relevance today. I am convinced that a special preparedness in these situations will make it easier for Christ to make himself heard.

Christ chided Jerusalem for not having recognised

the time when God came to save it (Lk 19,44). He also taught an appropriate parable.

'When you see a cloud in the western sky, at once you say: "It is going to rain" — and it does. And when you feel the south wind blowing, you say: "It is going to get hot" — and it does. Hypocrites! You can read the signs of the earth and the sky; why, then, don't you know the meaning of this present time?' (Lk 12,54-56)

Let us ask Christ for the grace to recognise the moment when it is upon us. May he grant that we respond before it passes. May we, when it happens to us, see clearly that 'This is the hour to receive God's favour; today is the day...!' (2 Cor 6,2)

Sitting at Jesus' feet

'Jesus entered a village where a woman named Martha welcomed him in her home. She had a sister named Mary, who sat down at the Lord's feet and listened to his teaching. Martha was upset over all the work she had to do, so she came and said, "Lord don't you care that my sister has left me to do all the work by myself? Tell her to come and help me!" The Lord answered her, "Martha, Martha! You are worried and troubled about many things, but only one is essential. Mary has chosen the right thing, and it will not be taken away from her".' (Lk 10,38-42)

Mary's devotion to Our Lord merited his special attention and love. If every day we take time off to remain silently in the presence of Christ, this may well become a favourable occasion for Christ to show himself. Teresa of Avila, for example, found her daily 'holy hour' of solitary prayer the setting for most of her spiritual experiences. St John of the Cross is very outspoken in indicating this as the

place where we meet Christ. When we are in solitude, God introduces us to divine things; through it
he leads us to perfect rest and peace and joins us to
himself in loving union. In solitary prayer we acquire
the disposition of mind that makes us sensitive to the
stirrings of the heavenly Spouse in our soul. Com-
menting on the Canticle of Canticles he says: 'To
accomplish so unusual a feat as uniting ourselves
with our divine Lover, we have to go outside.
Because we will not find him unless we are outside,
alone, waiting in solitude.'[15] Although it is not the
only occasion on which Christ manifests himself —
John of the Cross too had other experiences — we
may be sure that solitary prayer is an important and
genuine situation that can lead to 'disclosures'.

Sitting at Jesus' feet, Mary listened with great
admiration and her heart was filled with love. So we,
too, should quietly sit in his presence, pondering his
words and feeling in us a great desire to love him
ever more. We should not be anxious to formulate or
even to understand; we simply sit at his feet raising
our eyes to him, our hearts filled with love.

'Lord, I look up to you,
  up to heaven where you sit on your throne.
As a servant looks at his master,
  as a maid looks at her mistress,
  so we will keep looking to you, O Lord Our God,
  until you have mercy on us.'

(Ps 123,1-2)

'Lord, I have given up my pride.
  My eyes are not raised in arrogance.
I am not concerned with great matters
  or with subjects too difficult for me.
Instead, I am content and at peace.
As a child lies quietly in its mother's arms,
  so my heart is quiet in me.'

(Ps 131,1-2)

31

In ways that are difficult to describe, Christ will make us know that he is with us, that he loves us. Christ, says St John of the Cross, is wounded by love when he finds a person waiting for him in solitude. He will certainly respond.

Travelling together

'Two of Jesus' disciples were going to a village named Emmaus, about seven miles from Jerusalem. They were talking to each other about all the things that had happened. As they talked and discussed, Jesus himself drew near and walked along with them. They saw him, but somehow did not recognise him...

'He broke the bread and gave it to them. Then their eyes were opened and they recognised him, but he vanished from their sight. They said to each other, "Did we not feel a fire burning in us when he talked to us on the road and explained the Scriptures?".' (Lk 24,13-16; 30-32)

In this sketch of the 'journey' of the two disciples, Luke gave an image of a Christian's everyday life. Luke loved the symbolic implication of journeys. He depicted Jesus' passion as a 'going up to Jerusalem' (Lk 9,51; 13,22; 17,11; 19,11; etc). He linked the expansion of the early Church with the missionary journeys of St Paul. In the Acts of the Apostles he frequently called Christianity simply 'the Way' (Acts 9,2; 19,9; 19,23; 22,4; 24,14; etc). The journey of the disciples was, for Luke, an image of the life Christians lead after Jesus' death and resurrection.

The Gospels portray many meetings with Jesus, most of them replete with symbolic meaning. The specific aspect of this meeting is Jesus' presence as one of the disciples. He is not recognised until much later. While the disciples talk about Jesus, he is taking part in their conversation. He himself helps them understand Scripture and the words he spoke during his public life. He was in this way fulfilling his promise, 'Where two or three come together in my name, I am there with them' (Mt 18,20).

This is a situation which, I believe, is happening more frequently in our lives than we may be aware of. We may be visiting friends, we may be travelling with someone in a car, we may be talking with others at lunch break or attending an informal meeting. If we are speaking on matters concerning religion, if we open our hearts to one another and exchange our convictions and experiences, Christ will take part in that discussion. He may well speak to us through some of the things that are being said by others. His thoughts and ideas may be expressed in a new and meaningful fashion by one of our companions.

There need be nothing dramatic or spectacular about this. It may have little in common with shared prayer or the kind of charismatic meeting that shakes a place to its foundations (Acts 4,31). Instead, the setting may well be a small kitchen littered with the usual after-breakfast debris, a corner in a double-decker bus or a four-seat table in a self-service canteen. It may be just as plain and everyday as the cobble-stoned road from Jerusalem to Emmaus.

'God seems to have an instinct for revealing himself in what is most common. In the ordinary and undramatic dimensions of reality God lies hidden but in a way which allows his presence to burst through. Perhaps the very humility and simplicity of what is ordinary calms our complex fears and need for assurance. Perhaps the very prosaic nature of what is common serves to still our soul, makes us feel that we are on familiar ground and thus allows God to be manifest.'[16]

33

Yet within this ordinary situation Christ may speak. We can recognise his presence when we feel 'a fire burning in us when he talks' (Lk 24,32). If we learn to listen with our hearts, we can be aware of the moment when it happens. We know then that beyond the immediate persons surrounding us — or rather, through these persons — we are face to face with Christ himself. The realisation will fill us with awe and love. It will help us respond to Christ with new fervour.

Healed by his touch

'A man suffering from leprosy came to Jesus, knelt down, and begged him for help. "If you want to," he said, "you can make me clean." Jesus was filled with pity. He stretched out his hand and touched the leper. "I do want to," he answered. "Be clean!" At once the disease left the man and he was clean.' (Mk 1,40-42)

The leper referred to in this episode was, perhaps, a religious man. For many years he must have prayed that God might heal him; but nothing happened. It needed the touch of Jesus' hand to restore him to health. Only by kneeling down in front of Jesus, by humbling himself to this carpenter from Nazareth, did he receive his cure.

In the Church today the power of 'healing' is being rediscovered. There are reports of extra-ordinary happenings: dramatic cures of bodily illnesses, healings of psychological scars, transformations of character following on real conversion. Much of this takes place in the wake of the so-called charismatic movement.[17] Undoubtedly we are rediscovering here an experience that was present in early Christianity. Those who have experienced

God's healing in this way know they have been touched by his hand.

But, again, we need not seek the event of 'healing' only in such an unusual and, at times, emotional setting. Christ gave expression to his power of healing in the sacraments of Confession and the Anointing of the Sick. Christ knew we are in need of a mediator, a person who is sacramentally visible and who can act in his name. Unaided, we cannot rid ourselves of our inadequacies, our sins and imperfections. We require the direction of a spiritual guide and the authority of a priest who can forgive in Jesus' name.

It is not easy to accept the necessity of this mediation. It goes against our human nature to kneel before another person and ask for his help. Yet the willingness to do this, entrusting ourselves to the judgement of a person deputed by Christ, is required as a condition. We have to be like Bartimaeus, the blind man, who had such confidence in Jesus that he threw off his cloak and left it behind when making his way to Jesus (Mk 10,50). If we have such faith, God will certainly heal us through our spiritual director and confessor.

If we are open to the Spirit, we will know that Christ himself is acting upon us through his priest. 'Whoever listens to you listens to me' (Lk 10,16). 'What you permit on earth will be permitted in Heaven' (Mt 18,18). 'If you forgive people's sins, they are forgiven' (Jn 20,23). When the priest speaks the words of absolution, we shall feel the marvellous touch of Jesus' hand. We shall be filled with relief and joy, with a deep sense of gratitude that springs from love. We shall realise then what Jesus meant when he said about the sinful woman, 'I tell you, the great love she has shown proves that her many sins have been forgiven. But whoever has been forgiven little shows only a little love' (Lk 7,47). When he heals us he pours his love into our hearts (Rom 5,5).

Prayer on the cross

'It was about twelve o'clock when the sun stopped shining and darkness covered the whole country until three o'clock. And the curtain in the temple was torn in two. Jesus cried out in a loud voice, "Father! In your hands I place my spirit!" After these words he died.' (Lk 23,44-46)

Suspended from the cross, Jesus prayed to his Father. His prayers ranged from ordinary human despair — 'My God, my God, why did you abandon me?' (Mt 27,46) — to surrender in trust: 'Father! Into your hands I commend my spirit!' (Lk 23,46). The cries of Jesus from the cross reflect another aspect of our human life: our experience of God in suffering.

It almost seems a contradiction in terms, but God may be closer to us when he seems to abandon us. The validity of this assertion is confirmed by those who have gone through the experience in a special way. Walter J Ciszek was a Polish priest who was captured by the Russians during World War II and subjected to torture and imprisonment for 23 years. He recalls the despair he endured during the interrogations in Lubianka prison.

'One day the blackness closed in around me completely. Perhaps it was brought on by exhaustion, but I reached the point of despair. I was overwhelmed by the hopelessness of my situation. I knew that I was approaching the end of my ability. I could see no way out of it. Yes, I despaired in the most literal sense of the word: I lost all sense of hope.'

In the depth of his suffering he turned to God and pleaded for special help. During this prayer the thought of our Lord's agony in the garden suddenly brought him new hope and strength. The fact that

Jesus, too, had known the feeling of fear and weakness in his human nature filled him with a new sense of love. Jesus' submission to the will of his Father invited him to a similar, total self-surrender.

'What a wonderful treasure and source of strength and consolation our Lord's agony in the garden became for me from that moment on. I saw clearly what I must do. I can only call it a conversion experience, and I can only tell you frankly that my life was changed from that moment on.'[18]

Suddenly he had understood that he had to abandon himself totally to God's will. By adopting this spirit of self-abandonment he was able to bear loneliness, pain and torture with new strength. It had now been filled with meaning.

Simone Weil is another contemporary of ours who has left a valuable testimony on this matter. Being constantly plagued by severe headaches and violent depressions, she underwent a great deal of suffering. In the course of time she came to understand that, by a strange paradox, affliction itself can unite us to the love of God. She explains this with an image taken from the crucifixion.

All affliction, whether physical pain, anxiety of mind or social rejection, finds its expression in the nail used at the crucifixion. All the immensity of violence, brutal and blind to the extreme, is concentrated in it. It pierces the soul in its centre, highlighting the creature's infinite distance from God.

'He whose soul remains ever turned in the direction of God while the nail pierces it, finds himself nailed on to the very centre of the universe. It is the true centre, it is not in the middle, it is beyond space and time, it is God. In a dimension which does not belong to space, which is not time, which is indeed quite a different dimension, the nail has pierced a hole through all creation, through the thickness of a screen which separates the soul from God.'[19]

What happens is, she says, that the deepest moment of pain, paradoxically, can become the clearest moment of knowing the love of Christ. We are suddenly in touch with God in an inexpressibly real awareness.

It is not without reason that Christ travelled the human way of fear. humiliation, physical pain and death. When such experiences happen in our lives, they may become instruments of union with Christ. If from the depth of our affliction we cry out to him, if we stretch out our arms in despair, he will certainly reach down and comfort us in a tangible manner. He will gradually give us the strength and the peace of mind to carry our cross with love. 'We are even proud of our troubles, because we know that trouble produces patience, patience brings God's approval, and his approval creates hope. This hope does not disappoint us, for God has poured out his love into our hearts by means of the Holy Spirit, who is God's gift to us' (Rom 5,3-5).

Footwashing

'Jesus rose from the table, took off his clothes, and tied a towel round his waist. Then he poured some water into a basin and began to wash the disciples' feet and dry them with the towel round his waist... After Jesus had washed their feet, he put his clothes back on and returned to his place at the table. "Do you understand what I have just done to you?" he asked.' (Jn 13,4-5;12)

The disciples' feet were dirty. The hot weather, the dusty roads and their open sandals had made their feet black with sweat and filth. Before they could sit back and stretch themselves comfortably on the couches provided for the meal, their feet needed to be washed. Someone had to perform this service. Jesus decided to do it himself. Notwithstanding his status as 'rabbi' and his own tiredness, he took upon himself the laborious and humiliating task. In doing so, he set an example of selfless love.

It is interesting to note that converts in India have stated that they were attracted to Christianity most of all through the loving service rendered by priests and religious. It was not the intellectual superiority of Christian doctrine that fascinated them, but the mystery of a person 'wasting' his life to be of use to others. They did not understand at first why people from another country should come and bother about the outcasts, the poor, the hungry in their own villages. They saw in admiration how religious sisters gave themselves totally to the care of the old, the incurably diseased, the orphans and the handicapped. It only made sense to them when they discovered it was love; and in that love they recognised the love of Christ. For many Hindus, even for those who would not dream of becoming Christians, a person like Mother Teresa of Calcutta is a manifestation of God's love.

Christ said 'If you have love for one another, then everyone will know that you are my disciples' (Jn 13,35). We too come across this selfless love in other people. It may take a variety of forms. A girl may take a demanding job and work overtime to pay for the college studies of her younger brother. A man may spend his whole life looking after a bed-ridden wife who was crippled in an accident; he may do it joyfully so that she never discovers what it costs him. A young man turns his back on a promising career in his father's business to join a religious society. Some people are extremely generous and are always ready to help those in trouble. Even granted that much of people's 'charity' springs from mixed motives, we find plenty of examples of genuine 'Footwashing' if we have the eyes to see them.

When we witness such unselfish love, this may well become for us a 'disclosure' situation. This will all the more be so when we ourselves are the beneficiaries of such love. In the people who are kind to us, who serve us at their own expense, who wash our feet not because they have to do so, but only because they love us — in such people we meet Christ.

Breaking the bread

'Jesus looked up to heaven and said, "Father, the hour has come. Give glory to your Son, so that the Son may give glory to you. For you put him in charge of all mankind, so that he might give eternal life to all those you entrusted to him. And eternal life means knowing you, the only true God, and knowing Jesus Christ, whom you sent. I have shown your glory on earth. I have finished the work you gave me to do. Father! give me glory in your presence now, the same glory I had with you before the world was made".' (Jn 17,1-6)

At the Last Supper Christ formed his disciples into an intimate community. He spoke to them of the mutual love they should have for one another. He prayed for them in very personal words. He commanded them to break the bread together in his name. As C. H. Dodd has rightly pointed out, in John 13-17 Christ was not only talking *about* his future coming and his future eucharistic presence; the friendly gathering with the disciples, his prayer at the breaking of the bread already brought about his presence in anticipation. Here we find a complete model of Jesus' eucharistic presence. [20]

Jesus' long discussion with his disciples, the institution of the Eucharist, and his highpriestly prayer, form together the inspired model of Holy

Mass. The overriding theme of Jesus' words and actions is: unity. It was Jesus' purpose to show us how we can be one with himself and one with the Father. What will happen to Jesus' disciples when he has ascended to heaven? Jesus' answer is: 'Come together in my name, break the bread and drink the chalice in commemoration of me. Then I will be united with you.'

A eucharistic celebration sacramentalises Jesus' presence. He comes to us not only under the visual signs of bread and wine, in the symbolic separation of his body and blood. Jesus reveals himself through the event itself, through the group of disciples that relive the mysteries of his passion and resurrection in his memory. Jesus shows himself through the common concern, the love of the group.

C. Traets maintains that this is the way in which we have to understand Jesus' promise: 'I will reveal myself to you' (Jn 14,20). In his view, Jesus' return and Jesus' presence among the disciples can be known because Jesus' love can be seen at work in them. When looking at their brothers and sisters, the disciples perceive Jesus and the Father. It is an indirect perception, but a real one, says Traets, which has as its immediate object the ecclesial love experienced by the community.[21]

In the Catholic tradition of past centuries, great weight has been attached to the signs of bread and wine. In reaction to certain trends of the Reformation, the real presence of Christ under these symbols was stressed. In the life of prayer, expression was given to this belief in a great devotion to the personal reception of Holy Communion, in the encouragement of visits to the Blessed Sacrament and in paraliturgical functions in honour of the exposed sacramental sign. The kernel of what was being reaffirmed through these beliefs and practice was, no doubt, of great value. Jesus' real sacramental presence

41

under the sacred species remains an inalienable part of the eucharistic mystery.

But we may legitimately ask if this was all Jesus meant to do through the Eucharist; if this is a *complete* understanding of the eucharistic manifestation? After all, by themselves the bread and the wine cannot signify Jesus' presence. No visible change takes place in either of them in the course of their consecration. The consecrated species of bread and wine can only be recognised as such because they remain at the centre of the liturgical activity of the community.

The two disciples at Emmaus recognised Jesus 'at the breaking of the bread' (Lk 24,31.35). Christ will manifest himself to us, too, if we open our eyes to the full symbolism of the eucharistic celebration. We meet him in so many ways: in his word, in his priest, in his sacramental body and blood, in the 'church' of his followers. If he is present anywhere in our lives, he is present here in this sharing of prayers and symbols, celebrated in his memory.

Vision on the mountain

'Six days later Jesus took with him Peter and the brothers, James and John, and led them up a high mountain so that they could be alone. As they looked on, a change came over Jesus: his face began to shine like the sun, and his clothes became dazzling white. Then the three disciples saw Moses and Elijah talking with Jesus. So Peter spoke up and said to Jesus, "Lord how good it is that we are here!" ' (Mt 17,1-4)

The three apostles saw Jesus transfigured. They had what we would call today a 'peak experience'. For a short while they saw Jesus radiant with divine glory. To give them this vision of himself, Jesus took them to a secluded and carefully chosen place, the top of a high mountain. Jesus did not manifest himself in this way while he was sharing his daily food with them, while curing the sick in Capernaum, or while mingling with the crowds in the temple at Jerusalem. To reveal his radiance to them in this particular way, Jesus had to take them away from their everyday relationships and daily routine.

Contemplation requires withdrawal. Throughout the history of the Church there have been men and women who have sought to meet Christ in a more intimate way by a life lived in solitude and silence. The old contemplative orders flourish in our own days and new communities are springing up. Herbert Slade reports on a new Anglican initiative at the Anchorhold, Haywards Heath. This community has taken the mystery of the Transfiguration as its model of how a life of contemplation should be lived.[22]

Not all of us can join a contemplative order, but sometimes we can withdraw from everyday life by making a retreat. Such retreats have often proved an ideal setting for a deeper experience of God. Both Moses and Elijah saw God only after a forty-day fast. Ignatius of Loyola was converted during a prolonged illness that forced him to reappraise his life. Many persons have found God in 'the desert'.[23] God's words in Hosea may well be addressed to us: 'I am going to take you into the desert; there I will win you back with words of love' (cf Hos 2,14).

The meeting of love

I feel that my description of the various 'moments' when Christ may reveal himself, lacks their most important ingredient, namely the experience itself. Since this is a very personal thing, an intimate recognition, a meeting of love, it cannot be described. Provided we have the right disposition, Christ himself will step in and thereby change the whole situation into something living and unspeakable.

Wanting to see Christ is not a desire *we* have conceived, not an initiative *we* have taken. Christ promised he would reveal himself. It is he who is anxious to enter our lives in a visible manner. But, respecting our freedom, he wants us to remove first the obstacles we put in his way. Christ may well repeat to us what he said to the bishop of Laodicea: 'You say, "I am rich and well off; I have all I need." But you do not realise how miserable and pitiful you are! You are poor, naked and blind' (Rev 3,17). After telling us that, he rebukes us because he loves us, and advising us to put ointment on our eyes so that we may see, he gives us this wonderful assurance:

'Listen! I stand at the door and knock.
If anyone listens to my voice and opens the door,
I will enter his home and eat with him.
And he will eat with me.'

(Rev 3,20)

FOOTNOTES

Awareness of the suffering Christ

1. An early form of this meditation was published in the *Indian Journal of Theology* 24(1975) pp132-142.

2. Compare: D. H. MILLING, 'History and Prophecy in the Marcan Passion Narrative', *South Indian Journal of Theology* 16, (1967), pp42-53.

3. Ausonius, *Epigrammata*, 25.

4. The first recorded use is ascribed to Pope Boniface VIII (1303). It probably goes back to earlier Latin sources. D. J. A. WESTERHUIS, *Latijns Citaten Boek*, Spectrum, Utrecht 1957, p158.

5. Publius Syrus, *Sententia*; D. J. A. WESTERHUIS, l.c., p197.

6. For a summary of the opinion of the Fathers, see J. KNABEN-BAUER, *Evangelium Secundum Matthaeum*, Lethielleux, Paris 1892, pp470-471.

7. *Moralia*, Book 22, ch 12; here quoted after Thomas Aquinas, *Catena Aurea*, Vol II, Marietti, Turin 1925, p328.

8. Texts from: J. B. LIGHTFOOT, *The Apostolic Fathers*, Macmillan, London, 1898, re-edition by J. R. HARMER, pp141-142.

9. J. B. LIGHTFOOT, *The Apostolic Fathers*, Part II, Macmillan, London 1889, pp15-17 (introd); pp68-70 (commentary).

10. This silence is well described by Ch JOURNET in The *Dark Knowledge of God*, Sheed and Ward, London 1948.

11. K. RAHNER, *Encounters with Silence*, Sands, London, 1960, 1966 (11), pp19-25.

12. P. WATLAWICK, J. H. Beavin, D. Jackson, *Pragmatics of Human Communications*, New York 1967, ch 2, para 2.21.

13. 'The World Food Crisis' in *Time*, November 11 (1974), pp22-29, esp p25.

Recognise the moment

14. I published the contents of this chapter in a slightly different version in a book only available in India: *Come and See*, Theological Publications in India, Bangalore 1980, pp234-250.

15. *Dark Night of the Soul* Bk 2, ch 7,14; *Spiritual Canticle*, stropha 34; ed P. NAZARENO, *Opere di S Giovanni della Croce*, Postulazio Carmelitani, Roma 1959, pp478,745-746.

16. F. MARTIN, *Touching God*, Dimension Books, Denville 1975, p88.

17. Cf F. MACNUTT, *The Power to Heal*, Ave Maria Press, Notre Dame 1977.

18. W. J. CISZEK, *He Leadeth Me*, Doubleday Image Book, Garden City 1975, pp86-88.

19. S. WEIL, 'The Love of God and Affliction', *Waiting on God*, Fontana 1959, pp93-94.

20. C. H. DODD, *The Interpretation of the Fourth Gospel*, Cambridge University Press 1963, pp418-423.

21. C. TRAETS, *Voir Jésus et le Père en Lui selon l'Evangile de Saint Jean*, Universitas Gregoriana, Roma 1967, pp181-182; cf G. HIBBERT, *John*, Sheed & Ward, London 1972, p137.

22. H. SLADE, *Exploration into Contemplative Prayer*, Darton, Longman and Todd, London 1975.

23. Two excellent, contemporary reports on 'desert' experiences are: C. CARRETTO, *In Search of the Beyond*, Darton, Longman and Todd, London 1975; H. J. M. NOUWEN, *The Genesee Diary*, Doubleday, Garden City 1976.

NOTES

NOTES